Williamson **W** Publishing

Draw Your Own CARTOONS!

© 2000 Don Mayne

Don Mayne

Quick Starts for Kids!

WILLIAMSON PUBLISHING • CHARLOTTE, VERMONT

LIBRARY OF CONGRESS CATALOGING-IN-PUBLICATION DATA

Mayne, Don, 1961–
    Draw your own cartoons! / written and illustrated by Don Mayne.
        p. cm. — (A Williamson quick starts for kids book)
    Includes index.
    ISBN 1-885593-76-7 (pbk.)
        1. Cartooning—Technique—Juvenile literature. [1. Cartooning—Technique. 2.
Drawing—Technique. 3. Cartoons and comics.] I. Title. II. Series.

NC1320 .M34 2000
741.5—dc21   00-043484

Quick Starts for Kids!® series editor: **Susan Williamson**
Interior design: **Bonnie Atwater**
Illustrations: **Don Mayne**
Cover design: **Marie Doyle**
Cover illustrations: **Michael Kline**
Cover framed cartoons: **Don Mayne**
Printing: **Capital City Press**

WILLIAMSON PUBLISHING CO.
P.O. BOX 185
CHARLOTTE, VT 05445
(800) 234-8791

Manufactured in the United States of America

10 9 8 7 6 5 4

Dedication

To my family: to my daughter Fiona, who draws even better than I did at her age; to my son, Logan, who has a delightfully off-center sense of humor; and most of all to my wife, Monica, who has supported my work and made all of my dreams and ideas possible.

Acknowledgments

I would like to take a moment to thank all of the kids who ever took one of my cartoon courses. The ideas in this book evolved as a direct result of the creativity and enthusiasm we all shared in those classes. It was the kids who taught me about what makes young people laugh and also about the many great new cartoons that are being drawn for television these days. I know that someday I'll see their cartoons in the funny pages (or on TV)!

contents

Welcome to the Wacky World of Cartooning!

*I*f you wish you could capture funny moments in drawings that would make people smile or laugh, you already have what it takes to be a cartoonist hiding inside you — and it's time to let it out!

Take me, for example. Everywhere I look, I see something — a scene, a person, an animal — just waiting to be "cartoonified" (you'll see the world that way, too, after only a few pages of this book).

By the time I was 10 years old, I was doing lots of funny drawings. But I didn't just roll out of bed one morning and suddenly begin drawing professional-looking cartoons. Actually, I began by tracing my favorite cartoon characters — *Peanuts* by Charles Schultz and *B.C.* by Johnny Hart. Both of these comic strips have simple characters that are easy to draw.

It didn't take me long to figure out that these characters were easier to draw if I used circles and ovals to "build" them (like the three circles you would draw for a snowman) before I drew them with an ink pen. This technique is one of the most important cartooning secrets that I'll share with you in this book.

My first drawings were very rough, and I was frustrated at first by what I thought were "mistakes." Then, I realized that if I propped up those mistakes in front of me while I did my next drawing, I could learn from them! Now, I never throw away my mistakes. Instead, I let them help me.

With lots of practice, I improved my skills and developed my own style, and now I can draw just about anything I want to. I'd like to share what I know with all you budding cartoonists (yes, *you* are a cartoonist). So, here we go on an adventure to the land of grins, giggles, and good times ...

Don Mayne

DON! YOUR DINNER'S GETTING COLD, AGAIN!

Chapter 1

Ready! Set! Sharpen Those Pencils!

GRRRKKKK!

All you really need to be a cartoonist is a piece of paper (even the back of an already used one will do!) and a sharp pencil. But here are a few tips, tools, and techniques that make cartooning more fun and your drawings more professional-looking.

MATERIALS

For starters, here are a few things that all cartoonists keep in good supply:

 ★ **Good-quality pencils.**
Try to find pencils that sharpen easily, draw soft, clean lines, and have erasers on them that work. (Erasing is key to successful cartooning, as you'll see. I erase *lots* until I get what I want.) Dixon Ticonderoga #2 pencils are my favorites!

★ **A large art eraser.** Very handy for big rubouts and for cleaning up a finished drawing. You may want to try different brands to find one that erases without smearing or smudging

★ **Black felt- or plastic-tipped pens and markers.** Make sure the ink *really* is black! Either regular or permanent ink is fine.

★ **A clear, see-through ruler.** If you can see what's *underneath* the ruler, you'll find it a lot easier to use!

 ★ **Nontoxic correction fluid (like Liquid Paper).** This stuff is the cartoonist's best friend, as it greatly reduces the fear of failure! Make sure you get a nontoxic brand; we cartoonists need all our brain cells to produce good cartoons.

★ **Colored markers or colored pencils.**
You'll want a large assortment so you can add color to your favorite cartoons. Make sure the ones you choose produce clean, true colors!

★ **Paper — and lots of it!** Try lots of different kinds of paper until you find one that works best for *you!*

One of the best things about cartooning is that you don't need to buy any expensive materials!

Paper Particulars

For practice or rough drawings, use both sides of every sheet of paper. (And please recycle used paper.)

Here are some things to consider when selecting paper:

★ **Heavy, stiff "card" stock.** Doesn't wrinkle when you erase.

★ **Smooth-surface paper.** You can draw very light pencil marks on it.

★ **Nonporous paper.** Black ink won't soak in or "bleed" (spread) too much.

★ **Standard-size paper.** Easy to copy, print, or mail!

★ **Illustration board** is a very nice surface for final drawings. It's available at art supply stores, but you'll have to cut it into smaller pieces.

A great cartoon takes lots of erasing, even for the pros! Be patient, and don't be afraid to experiment!

TRACING

Fun Practice for Every Cartoonist!

Just like anything else that you want to become really good at, cartooning takes practice. But — get this — practicing cartooning is fun!

When I was learning to draw cartoons, I would practice by tracing my favorite cartoons carefully and patiently. When you practice the methods below, think about how your fingers move to trace over the lines under your paper. It's a lot like learning to write your name — eventually, your fingers will know just what to do!

METHOD #1 Window Tracing

To trace very easily, first tape whatever you want to trace to a bright window. Then, tape your paper over it. Remember to press *lightly* with your pencil so it's easy to erase — and so you don't break the window!

PSSST! *Quick Starts* CARTOONING SECRETS . . .

Tracing helps you realize that YOU control the pencil!

REMEMBER: Don't write in this book. Practice *tracing* when you want to use a shape!

METHOD #2 ## The Three-Step "Magic Rub"

If your paper or illustration board is too thick to see through, the "magic rub" is an excellent way to transfer the images.

1 Trace the image using regular tracing paper.

2 Turn the tracing paper over and rub a smooth layer of pencil lead *behind* the image, rubbing back and forth with the pencil lying almost flat.

Rub back and forth

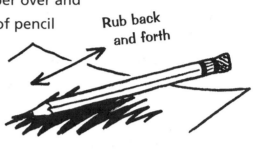

3 Put the tracing paper right side up on your thick (opaque) paper and retrace over the lines of your image. Presto! The image will be transferred onto the new paper!

METHOD #3 ## Tracing Objects

Need a circle? Try tracing a jar lid, a coin, or anything round! You can do the same for other shapes.

Start a collection of objects that can be traced for cool shapes. How about some dice, a fingernail file, or a small six-sided box?

Can you turn those shapes into a wacky drawing?

Maybe your circle becomes a goofy face, like this:

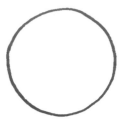

Trace a coin.

Sketch in a few goofy shapes.

Add some details …

Hey! A silly face!

Trace a paper clip.

Add one line and four hot-dog shapes …

… and you've made an arm with a hand!

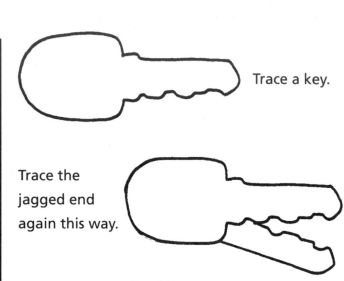

Trace a key.

Trace the jagged end again this way.

Add a few details …

… and you've got a scary alligator head!

Now, you try it! Practice that pencil control so that pretty soon your pencil will seem to draw what's pictured in your mind — almost by itself!

Chapter 2

From Head to Toe:
Body Types and Facial Expressions

What's your favorite part of a cartoon? The funny people, of course!

Now, can you draw a circle? How about a triangle? Even a hot dog?

Then, you're well on your way to drawing cartoon figures! It's true — their

heads and bodies start with simple shapes that give them their "character."

Then, you can pick and choose from our gallery of faces (can you guess

the most important facial features a cartoonist draws?), hairstyles,

hands, and feet to create a unique personality for each

one — from grumpy to silly to just plain wacky!

Let's see how a cartoon figure "takes shape."

In pencil, draw a ...

Circle   **Triangle**   **Oval**   **Rectangle**

Trace these shapes if you prefer. Add more shapes or tilt a shape, however you like. (It's always *your* choice in cartooning.)

And turn them into these!

PSSST! Quick Starts CARTOONING SECRETS . . .

If you can draw *basic shapes* like a circle, a square, and a triangle, then you're on your way to drawing cartoons just like the pros!

Giving Your Shapes Character!

CARTOON FACE PARTS

By tracing shapes (see page 8), you can build thousands of different character faces, mixing combinations of head shapes, hairstyles, eyes, mouths, and other features.

HEADS UP!

To practice drawing heads, start by tracing these!

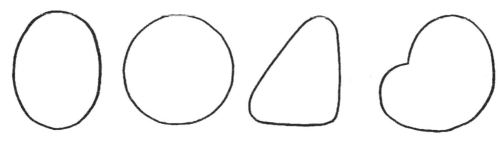

Or, create your OWN styles!

STYLIN' HAIR

Here are some to try. (You also can copy others from magazines.)

MAKING FACES

The Better to SMELL You With! ----------

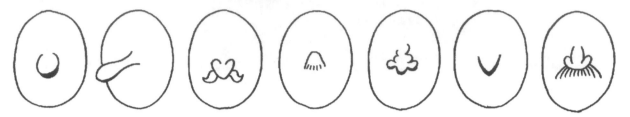

The Better to HEAR You With! ----------

The Better to SEE You With! ----------

The Better to EAT You With! ----------

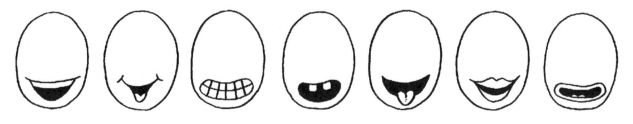

Draw Your Own Cartoons!

If you could draw only two facial features to express your cartoon character's emotions, eyes and a mouth would be the ones!

Now, ready to put all these face parts together? Before you start drawing, think about the mood your character is in. Now, start by tracing a head. Next, move your paper to a pair of eyes and trace those. Then, trace a nose, and so on. (If you trace a feature and your character suddenly doesn't look the way you want it to, just erase, and try something different.)

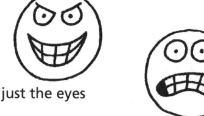

just the eyes

See how changing

or the mouth ... changes the character's whole personality?

Don't Forget the EYEBROWS!

Cartoonists use eyebrows very carefully to change a character's expression.

If you really want to see what I mean, try drawing the expressions (on page 16) *without* eyebrows.

One of the best ways to see eyebrows change — and to learn how to draw them — is to trace expressions you like from comic books. Then, study how the eyebrows are drawn.

Talking Heads

Can you match each face to one of these words?

Painful, Annoyed, Determined, Surprised, Nervous, Greedy, Wacky, Angry, Happy, Obnoxious, Grumpy, Complaining, Upset, Sick, Dizzy, Scared

Trace some of these faces for practice. (Remember that old "pencil control.")

Then, when you're ready, make up your own!

ANSWERS: 1. Angry, 2. Annoyed, 3. Complaining, 4. Determined, 5. Dizzy, 6. Greedy, 7. Grumpy, 8. Happy, 9. Nervous, 10. Obnoxious, 11. Painful, 12. Scared, 13. Sick, 14. Surprised, 15. Upset, 16. Wacky

Draw Your Own Cartoons!

"One Look Is Worth a Thousand Words!"

★ Pick one of the faces shown on page 16 and make a list of all the words you can think of to describe the expression.

★ Draw one of these faces and show it to a friend. Can she guess what the expression is?

★ Play "Which Face?" (below) and match up the faces with these questions. Now, you try making up questions to match the remaining faces!

Which face looks as if he just got off a wild ride at an amusement park?

Which face looks mean and scary?

Which face looks like your dad when you give him a big hug for no reason in particular?

Which face looks like your teacher when he catches you passing a note to your friend?

Which face looks like your older sister when she realizes you've borrowed something of hers without asking?

Which face looks like your mom when you clean your room without being asked?

Which face looks like you when you eat too much cake?

PSSST! Quick Starts CARTOONING SECRETS . . .

A great way to create new funny faces is to goof around in front of the mirror. Then, draw what you see and feel!

ANSWERS: dizzy, angry, happy, grumpy, annoyed, surprised, sick

BODY BUILDING — Is Your Character a HOT DOG or a PEAR?

The next thing your character needs is a body. So it's back to basic shapes again! You can create lots of different body types by drawing the shapes of common foods. (Okay, the heart isn't a food, but it's a great cartooning shape!)

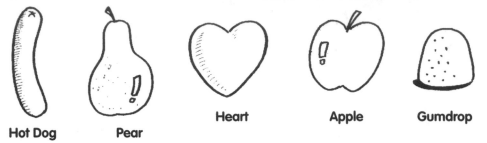

Hot Dog **Pear** **Heart** **Apple** **Gumdrop**

Decide what you want your character to look like, focusing on the message you want to communicate. Heavyset or lean? Tall or short? Strong or weak? Pick a food shape that best illustrates this type and combine it with the other basic shapes you drew earlier.

See how the shape of the body type adds to the character?

Try some other shapes to use, too. How about "Egg Man"? Let me show you step-by-step how to build a character using food shapes — in this case, an egg!

1. Start with an egg shape. (An egg is an oval that's a little pointier at one end.)

2. Let's use a circle — perhaps an orange — for his head.

3. Hot-dog shapes are good for arms. See how they start at the shoulders?

One arm is partially hidden behind the body.

4. Put some circles (like grapes) at the end of his arms for hands. For thick legs, draw shapes like soup cans — one slightly in front of the other. Bean shapes make good feet.

5. You can even use the basic shapes of food to draw some of the finer details! Can you tell what these food shapes are?

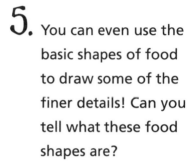

6. Okay, so here's "Egg Man," with all of his food shapes. (Are you hungry yet?) Notice that all the pencil lines are showing, so you can see the whole shape. Some of these lines won't be part of the final picture. The trick is to sketch every-thing *lightly* in pencil first, then ink over the final lines. I'll show you how to do this on pages 32–34.

He's a BANANA, for sure!

Open that refrigerator or better yet, imagine you are walking down the fresh fruit and vegetable aisle at the grocery store. Which food shapes would you use for these characters' basic body shapes?

Fullback on the football team

Champion diver

Olympic gymnast

"Stars on Ice" ice skater

Award-winning couch potato

Fat-free fanatic

Do a quick sketch and see what works for *you*.

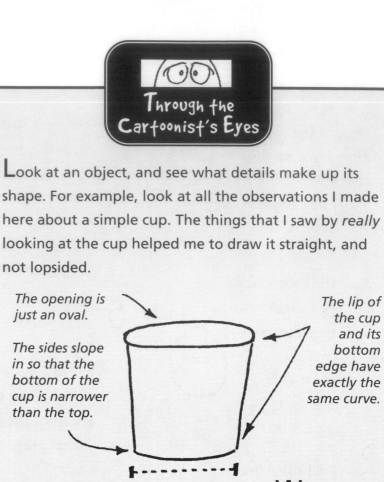

Through the Cartoonist's Eyes

Look at an object, and see what details make up its shape. For example, look at all the observations I made here about a simple cup. The things that I saw by *really* looking at the cup helped me to draw it straight, and not lopsided.

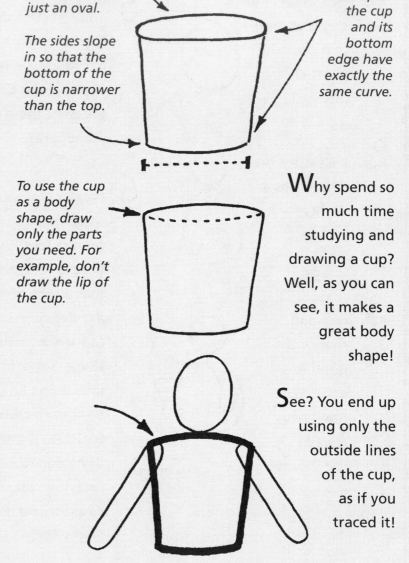

The opening is just an oval.

The sides slope in so that the bottom of the cup is narrower than the top.

The lip of the cup and its bottom edge have exactly the same curve.

To use the cup as a body shape, draw only the parts you need. For example, don't draw the lip of the cup.

Why spend so much time studying and drawing a cup? Well, as you can see, it makes a great body shape!

See? You end up using only the outside lines of the cup, as if you traced it!

For hands, bring on enough hot dogs for a barbecue!

1. Begin with an oval.

2. Sketch hot-dog shapes for fingers.

Draw the thumb about halfway up the side of the oval.

Separate the fingers a little.

3. Erase a few lines as shown.

The thumb should be slightly curved. Also, add a small curved line to show the "ball" of the thumb.

FOOT STOMPIN'

1. Start with a long egg shape.

2. Add small ovals for the toes (one bigger for the "big toe").

3. Overlap the toes and add a small curved line on the bottom.

Feet from the side:

Cartoon characters usually only have three fingers. Why? Because it's one less finger to draw! (Cartoonists are basically lazy.)

Through the Cartoonist's Eyes

Hands are very important for showing expression and action. Can you tell what these hands are "saying"?

  *PSSST!* Quick Starts CARTOONING SECRETS . . .

There is no such thing as TOO much practice if you want to draw really good hands and feet! Fortunately, most everybody has a few to use as models, especially the one that isn't holding the pencil!

Chapter 3

Dressing Your Character

*F*rom a baseball cap to big, baggy jeans to your favorite style of
sneakers, clothes really do make the cartoon character! And they're
not hard to draw (you guessed it — it's back to basic shapes).
And for the finishing touch, toss in a prop like a lacrosse stick or a
TV remote, and everyone will know at a glance whether your
character is a star athlete or a couch potato!

CLOTHES and PROPS

Now, here's where you can really create personality! Have you ever seen Charlie Brown dressed in anything other than his shirt with the zigzag stripe? Does Linus go anywhere without his blanket draped over his shoulder? How about you? Do you have a favorite hat you always wear that people associate with you?

C A P S
and Assorted Headgear!

You can personalize caps and helmets by giving them decals and insignia of local teams and famous places.

The Perfect Baseball Cap

1. Draw a half circle with a curved line on the bottom.

2. Draw another curved line for the bill of the cap.

3. Then, just extend the bottom of the cap!

A Bike Helmet

1. Draw a half circle.

2. Add a curved line to make a moon shape.

3. Add details, like chin straps or cool decorations and decals.

The Ski Cap

1. Draw a half circle.

2. Make a thick "hot dog" at the bottom.

3. Draw some vertical lines inside the cap.

A Sports Helmet

1. Draw a half circle.

2. Add a smaller half circle on the bottom.

3. Draw a straight line that extends out, like this.

4. Finish the details by adding the top of the bill, and an air-hole at the ear.

5. Add some decorations and team decals.

The Funky Sideways Cap

1. Draw a half circle with a curved line on the bottom.

2. Make a point at the top, like the roof of a house.

3. Draw a wavy line for the bill of the hat.

4. Draw a "folded" line on the bottom of the bill.

Make sure your character wears it sideways!

Different-Styled "T"-SHIRTS

The Basic "" Shirt

1. Draw a line like waves on water.

2. Put a box end on each side for the sleeves.

3. Another big box end on the bottom will finish the job!

The Tank Top

 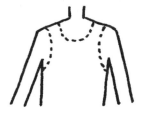 

1. Draw a body, using basic shapes.

2. Add curved lines at the neck and shoulders.

3. Add a number and it's a sports jersey!

PSSST! Quick Starts CARTOONING SECRETS . . .

Sit around with some friends and see if you can come up with one character prop or piece of clothing that you all associate with someone you know or a character in a book or TV show. Here are some to get you started:

Mary Poppins   Your science teacher

A character from *Sesame Street*   A chef

PANTS:
Long, Short, Baggy, and Tight

1. Basic pants start with an upside-down V.

2. Draw parallel lines (to the V) on the outside.

3. Close off the waist and the bottoms of the legs.

4. Add cuffs or ruffles to make different styles of pants.

To draw shorts, just show the legs poking out.

For baggy pants, make the upside-down V a lot lower, and show the cuffs all bunched up at the bottom. The shoes should be partially covered.

For tight pants, make sure the legs are narrower at the ankles.

 PSSST!

Quick Starts CARTOONING SECRETS . . .

The easiest way to draw a clothed cartoon figure is to draw the clothes *first*. Then, draw the arms, legs, and head poking out of them!

DRESSES: Just Another Body Shape

The basic dress is just a T-shirt with a lamp-shade shape (for the skirt) added on the bottom. Then, draw the legs poking out.

A DRESS CAN BE A **LARGE** SIZE, FOR A LARGE BODY TYPE...

...OR IT CAN BE SMALL AND SKINNY!

Through the Cartoonist's Eyes

One of the most fun things about drawing cartoons is designing your character's clothes. Look in store windows, magazines, and catalogs for ideas of what's "in" and what's not. Then, think of what your character would spend her money on — and dress her in what she would buy for herself!

JACKETS: What's the Weather Like?

A regular jacket is like a long-sleeved shirt, with a line down the middle for a zipper or buttons.

In really cold weather, the jacket gets a little puffier. See how the zipper gets crooked?

If it's really, *really* cold, your character could be all bundled up (look familiar?).

SHOES:
Easier Than Drawing Toes!

Shoes can add a nice "finishing touch" to your character!

For a shoe seen from the side, start by drawing a "bean" shape.

If you're looking at the shoe from the front, it looks more like a gumdrop shape.

    **A Cool Athletic Shoe**

1. Show which end has toes in it.

2. Draw the shoelaces.

3. Add a cool design or logo.

4. Draw a bumpy bottom.

A Fancy Shoe

1. Draw a line to show the bottom.

2. Add a strap and color it black.

1. Define the toe area and the bottom.

2. Add a decoration.

PSSST!

Quick Starts CARTOONING SECRETS . . .

If you show a little of the bottom of the shoe, it will look as if your character is walking.

Try different shoe styles!

CHARACTER PROPS

The trick with drawing props is to just draw enough so people can recognize the object at a glance.

Draw Your Own Cartoons!

Chapter 4

Creating a Cast of Characters:
Putting It All Together

Wow! You've learned to draw a lot! You have now what it takes to fill

a whole cartoon strip with people. You're ready for me to reveal my

secret method for creating each character — the step-by-step

techniques I use every time I sit down to draw a new cartoon figure

from start to finish. You'll have to read on to discover my formula —

all that I'll tell you here is that it's as easy as P.I.E!

Practice + P.I.E. = Perfect

How do you put all this together into a cartoon character? Easy! Just apply the **P.I.E.** formula to create your own cartoon character!

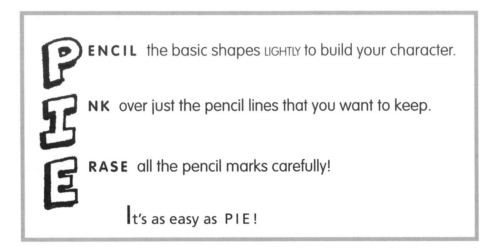

PENCIL the basic shapes LIGHTLY to build your character.

INK over just the pencil lines that you want to keep.

ERASE all the pencil marks carefully!

It's as easy as P I E !

Okay, now I'm going to show you step-by-step how to apply the **P.I.E.** formula, so that you can draw your character in any position! Remember to be patient — don't expect your drawings to be perfect from the get-go.

Use your pencil to lightly sketch the "plan" for where you will draw the final ink lines. Your pencil lines need to be made without pressing hard, so that they will be easy to erase when you're done. Now, ready to draw a dude on a skateboard?

PSSST! *Quick Starts* CARTOONING SECRETS . . .

In order for the P.I.E. formula to work, you must practice drawing VERY LIGHT pencil lines that are easy to erase! Got it? Good!

STEP 1: Pencil in the Basic Shapes

Sketch the *basic shapes* of your character's body **very lightly**, using pencil. Your goal is to establish your character's pose and to show what your character is doing.

STEP 2: Pencil in Clothes and Features

Sketch the outline of the clothes your character is wearing and the facial expression. Use hot-dog shapes to build your character's hands. If you need to erase unnecessary pencil marks to see better, go right ahead.

I added:

Eyes, nose, mouth, and ears

T-shirt sleeves

Vest

Hot-dog fingers

Details on shorts

Some details on shoes

STEP 3: Pencil in Props and Important Details

Still drawing lightly, sketch in the props your character is using. Make sure they look like your character is actually using them. See how you are defining who your character is? Erase gently and redraw until the props look the way you want them to look.

I added:

Helmet

Hair

Pupils in eyes

Teeth

Ear details

Elbow pads

Knee pads

Skateboard

More shoe details

Skateboard

STEP 4: Pencil in the Final Touches

Now, take time to look over your drawing. Check to see that all the details are the way you want them (see how I made his arms skinnier?).

Your goal is to have as complete a pencil drawing as possible, so that using the ink pen is easy.

Don't worry about extra pencil lines. You won't draw them in ink, and you're going to erase everything soon.

Can you see what else I added?

STEP 5: Ink Over ONLY the Lines You Want to Keep

Don't ink the pencil lines under the helmet, for example.

Ink around the outside lines only, just like tracing your hand on a piece of paper.

STEP 6: Erase ALL the Pencil Marks

Important! Make sure the ink is completely dry before you try to erase. Hold the paper down firmly and rub *gently* over the whole drawing with your eraser. If there are any marks left, go back over them with a smaller eraser. You can then ink in some texture or shading.

Now you have a finished drawing that looks as if you drew it perfectly the first time!

Bringing Your Character To "LIFE!"

Well, my friend, you are well on your way to creating your very own cartoon characters.

R E M E M B E R :

- ☆ Pencil control (tracing and practice)
- ☆ Expressing emotions and character
- ☆ Basic shapes
- ☆ P.I.E. formula

Now, let's develop your cartoon character!

First, think about your character's personality, interests, and behavior. Then, use different body shapes, face parts, clothes, and props to express these.

Let's develop an adventurous character together. What characteristics and props would make someone say, "Hmm ... this person obviously is about to set off on an adventure." Start by sketching the basic shapes and pose that might illustrate an adventurous character.

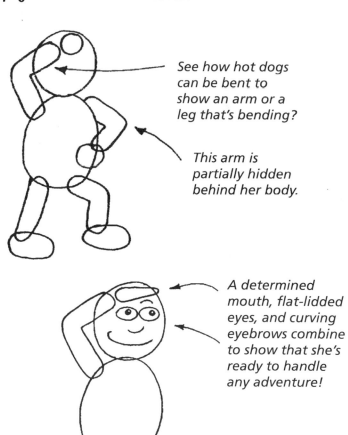

See how hot dogs can be bent to show an arm or a leg that's bending?

This arm is partially hidden behind her body.

A determined mouth, flat-lidded eyes, and curving eyebrows combine to show that she's ready to handle any adventure!

How about an adventurer's hat?

Don't forget the hands — they are part of the expression, too.

What might a person on an adventure be holding?

Lots of pockets are useful on an adventure.

Rugged boots make her look rugged, too!

Through the Cartoonist's Eyes

Okay, let me take you step-by-step through using all these things to show your character's personality ... only this time, **YOU** do all the drawing! I'll ask you a series of questions, and you "sketch" the answers on a sheet of paper. Here we go:

✯ *What do you want your character to be?*
A scaredy-cat

✯ *What kind of body would this person have?*
A skinny body

✯ *What kind of situation might this person be in?*
Scared of his own shadow

✯ *What kind of body position would indicate your character's personality?*
Jumping in fright

✯ *What expression and features would he or she have?*
Big, round eyes; high, arched eyebrows; wide-open mouth; hair standing on end; hands like claws

Now use the same questions to think of another character ... and another ... and another! Pretty soon, you'll have the cast of an entire cartoon strip!

Chapter 5

"Cartoonifying" Objects and Animals

So now you can draw all kinds of cool cartoon characters. But let's say you want to show one reading a book or riding a bike. No problem — just fire up the "cartoonifier"! This special machine turns normal (boring) objects into objects as funny as your cartoon people! Let's see how to use it.

"CARTOONIFYING"

Imagine that all cartoon objects pass through a special machine.

Normal boring object goes in …

Funny cartoon object comes out!

the "CARTOONIFIER"

Notice how the "cartoonifier" sometimes adds details (like the antenna on the TV). That adds interest.

PSSST!

Quick Starts CARTOONING SECRETS . . .

The secret to drawing cartoons can be summed up in one question: "If it isn't funny, why bother?" In cartoons, every object is part of your "cartoon fantasy world." So, why draw an ordinary object when you can make it look funny?

An ordinary house

A cartoon house

Let's look inside the "CARTOONIFIER" to see how it works:

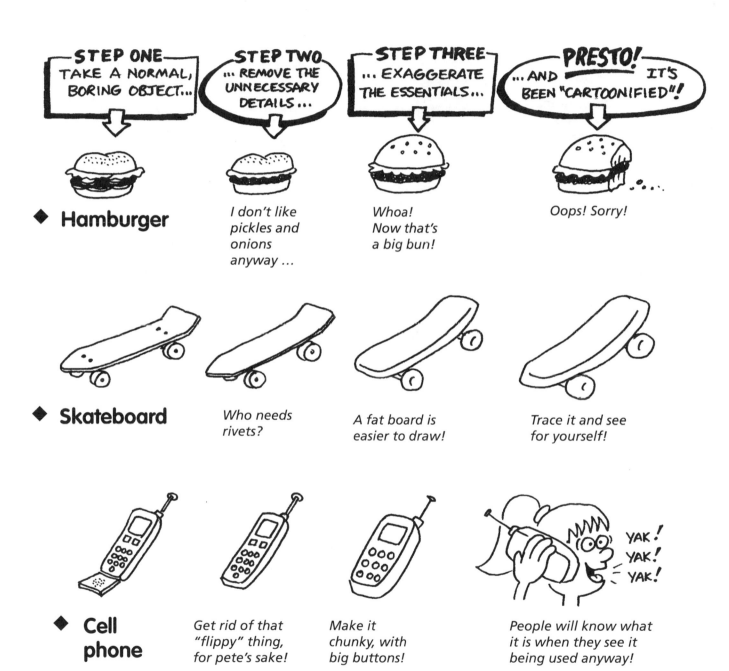

STEP ONE — TAKE A NORMAL, BORING OBJECT...

STEP TWO ... REMOVE THE UNNECESSARY DETAILS...

STEP THREE ... EXAGGERATE THE ESSENTIALS...

...AND **PRESTO!** IT'S BEEN "CARTOONIFIED"!

◆ **Hamburger**

I don't like pickles and onions anyway ...

Whoa! Now that's a big bun!

Oops! Sorry!

◆ **Skateboard**

Who needs rivets?

A fat board is easier to draw!

Trace it and see for yourself!

◆ **Cell phone**

Get rid of that "flippy" thing, for pete's sake!

Make it chunky, with big buttons!

People will know what it is when they see it being used anyway!

YAK! YAK! YAK!

The "Cartoonifier" Instruction Manual

1. Look at an ordinary bike. What are the things that show people that this object is a bike?

2. Draw the object as you see it, using (what else?) basic shapes.

3. Now, erase and redraw the lines, exaggerating those things that people will see and use to identify the object.

Start by making the wheels fatter (and leave out the spokes).

BEFORE:
AFTER:

4. Keep only the most essential details.

5. Maybe add something more interesting — just for the fun of it!

Make the other essential parts larger: the seat, the handle bars, and the pedal (one pedal is enough).

Use a simple double line for the frame and draw just a few spokes.

That's it!

"CARTOONIFYING" ANIMALS

Cartoonists have used animals for characters since, well, since cartooning began! Animals are fun to draw — and funny to look at. Plus, through animals you can express important feelings without offending anyone.

How do you start to draw a cartoon animal? You guessed it! You use those basic shapes! Most animals are made up of shapes that are easy to draw.

When you design a cartoon character based on an animal, you can exaggerate its features to emphasize its personality.

Owls are WISE.

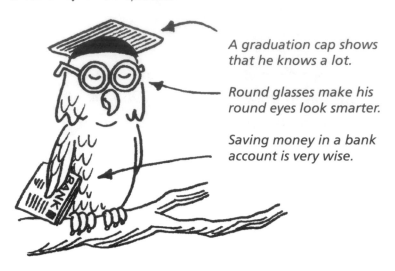

A graduation cap shows that he knows a lot.

Round glasses make his round eyes look smarter.

Saving money in a bank account is very wise.

Kittens are PLAYFUL.

A frisky tail makes her look very playful.

Large eyes show that she's looking for fun.

She plays with portable video games when nobody's looking.

Foxes are SLY.

The ears lying back means he's up to no good.

Mean eyes and a smiling mouth are a "sly" combination.

The tail between his legs shows he's sneaky (or that he's been naughty).

Chapter 6

Special Effects and Tricks of the Trade

*W*ow! You're well on your way to creating a complete cartoon that tells a story with a picture (and few or no words). Cartoonists use lots of secret tricks and special techniques to express things like motion, texture, intense emotion — even sounds! Let's see how to bring your cartoons to life!

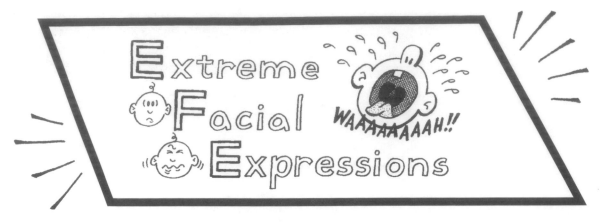

To make a cartoon memorable, s-t-r-e-t-c-h the facial expressions to amazing extremes!

Fright

Anger

Happiness

Quick Starts CARTOONING SECRETS . . .

 PSSST!

Drawing the mouths and eyes impossibly large will exaggerate the expressions. What else do you notice that I exaggerated?

CARTOON BODY LANGUAGE

Take a closer look at some funny cartoons. What makes them funny? You'll find it's often the characters' **REACTIONS** to things happening around them that make you laugh. Here are a few for starters:

See how you can tell the different moods and responses of the characters even though they have no facial expressions? If you were to add thought balloons to these body shapes, what would they be saying? (See below for possible answers.)

Through the Cartoonist's Eyes

A person's body often "speaks" before she even utters a single word. That's why it's called body language. And some of the funniest situations occur when someone says one thing, but his body says something completely different. Watch your friends or your family and you'll see what I mean — and discover the secret of drawing hilarious cartoons.

"Hey! I did it!"   "Now look what you've done!"   "Sorry, I don't feel like playing today."

Personally, this is my <u>favorite</u> part! Cartoonists use many different visual tricks to indicate action or movement in a cartoon. Here are a few examples that will stir things up and get things moving!

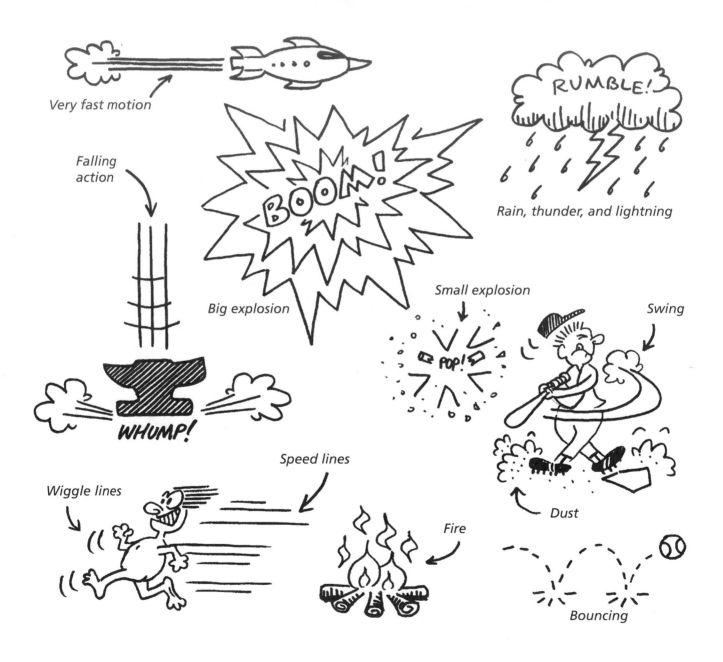

Very fast motion

Falling action

Big explosion

WHUMP!

RUMBLE!

Rain, thunder, and lightning

Small explosion

POP!

Swing

Dust

Wiggle lines

Speed lines

Fire

Bouncing

CARTOON FIGURES ON THE "MOVE"!

Because cartoon drawings don't actually move (unlike a cartoon character on TV), a cartoonist creates the illusion, or visual impression, of movement.

The Classic Run

Legs and arms are opposite each other and bent.

"Wiggle lines" indicate motion.

Feet are curved.

Shadow on the ground indicates the figure is in mid-air.

Hair is streaked out in a straight line.

"Zoom lines" indicate the figure is moving fast.

The back is arched, and the figure is leaning back.

Dust clouds, another common symbol, indicate fast motion.

TRY TO DRAW <u>YOUR OWN</u> CHARACTER IN THIS RUNNING POSITION!

 PSSST! *Quick Starts* CARTOONING SECRETS . . .

The tricks that cartoonists use to show motion are like a secret language. And here's the really cool part: Everyone understands this language without having it explained to them!

See how capturing a figure in its most active pose makes the drawing more exciting. Try making a commotion of motion using these examples:

The Dive

The Swing

SWISH!

BOOT!

The Classic "Boot"

The "Jump for Joy"

SHOOP!

The Classic "Fall"

The Dance

The Jump

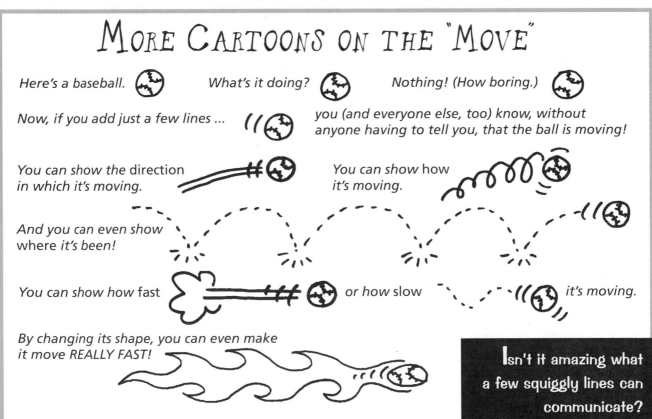

MORE CARTOONS ON THE "MOVE"

Here's a baseball.

What's it doing?

Nothing! (How boring.)

Now, if you add just a few lines ...

you (and everyone else, too) know, without anyone having to tell you, that the ball is moving!

You can show the direction in which it's moving.

You can show how it's moving.

And you can even show where it's been!

You can show how fast

or how slow

it's moving.

By changing its shape, you can even make it move REALLY FAST!

Isn't it amazing what a few squiggly lines can communicate?

Draw Your Own Cartoons!

CARTOON SPECIAL EFFECTS

(Hold this title upside down in a mirror!)

One of the most enjoyable things about drawing (and reading) cartoons is the great number of <u>visual clues</u> (sometimes called "special effects") that emphasize particular emotions, thoughts, or feelings. Here are just a few:

Good music

Bad music

Greed

Dizziness

Crying

Innocence

Snoring

Mean looks

Nervousness

Hot and spicy tastes

Love

Shock

Can you think of any more?

HOW ABOUT "CLOUD" EFFECTS?

A big fight   A bright idea   Cold

CARTOON SOUND EFFECTS

POW   ZOOOOM!!!   BANG!   SPLOOSH   BOINK!!   WHAM!   DING DONG   BOOM!   CRASH!   BEEP BEEP!   SPLAT   ZIP!

OTHER SPECIAL EFFECTS

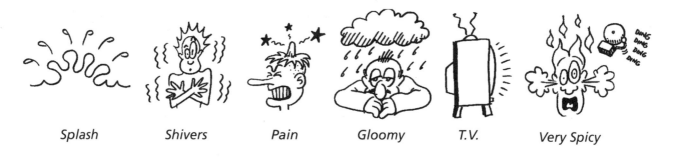

Splash   Shivers   Pain   Gloomy   T.V.   Very Spicy

PSSST! Quick Starts CARTOONING SECRETS . . .

With special effects, you can save drawing time and still communicate to your audience. You can also communicate to other people who speak different languages!

Adding textures is the way professionals add visual interest to their work.

Hatch Marks

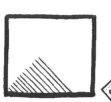  

Shading textured to look like fur

Crosshatch

Hatch marks

"Crazyhatch"

Bubbles

Crosshatch for fabric pattern

Zigzag

Dots

Straight lines

Bricks

Many of the textures you just learned work very well as shading. Or, invent some new ones to express your "shady" side!

YOU CAN EVEN "Cartoonify" LETTERS!

The way that you draw (yes, I said "draw") your letters when you put words in a cartoon has a lot to do with the way your words are interpreted. That's because it's not **WHAT** you say, but **HOW** you say it that counts!

How to "CARTOONIFY" LETTERS!

1. Sketch the letters LIGHTLY in pencil. Make sure you don't crowd them because you will be working with each letter.

CARTOONS

2. Still working lightly in pencil, shape the letters around the pencil lines until you have even, well-shaped letters.

CARTOONS

CARTOONS

3. Carefully ink the outline of the letters, drawing over the pencil lines that look best. Erase the pencil lines.

4. Use correction fluid to correct any mistakes, and add special effects if you want. You can make shadow letters by imagining that a light is shining on them from a specific direction.

Did you know that you can emphasize words by making them **BOLD** or *SLANTED*?

 BLOCK LETTERS make your words look more dramatic, and SHADOW LETTERS work even better!

 YOU CAN MIX ALL THE LETTERS UP AND MAKE THE WORDS LOOK CRAZY!!

 You can even draw the letters in your cartoon so they indicate the emotions or the character's tone of voice. *Soft*, LOUD, Casual, or WHISPER

YOU CAN EVEN MAKE YOUR CHARACTERS TALK FAST BY NOT PUTTING ANY SPACES BETWEEN THE LETTERS!

Cartoon speech and thought balloons are used to show what the characters are saying or thinking. Making the effort to plan and draw the lettering properly will make your cartoons look very professional!

 *Quick Starts* CARTOONING SECRETS . . .

 **I**f you draw the balloon FIRST, you might crowd the lettering:

 So ... draw the words first. Then, make a balloon that fits.

1 First, write out exactly what your character is going to say (on scrap paper).

CARTOON LETTERING IS EASY IF YOU TAKE THE TIME TO ~~PLAN~~ PLAN AND DO IT NEATLY!

2 Using a ruler, pencil light, straight lines to guide your lettering.

3 Pencil the lettering (don't forget to keep it LIGHT), making sure the words are spaced evenly.

CARTOON LETTERING IS EASY
IF YOU TAKE THE TIME TO
PLAN AND DO IT NEATLY!

4 Sketch the balloon's shape LIGHTLY in pencil. Make sure it's big enough. The "tail" of the balloon points to the character who is speaking (it doesn't have to go all the way into the mouth).

CARTOON LETTERING IS EASY
IF YOU TAKE THE TIME TO
PLAN AND DO IT NEATLY!

5 Ink the balloon and lettering neatly and erase the pencil marks.

CARTOON LETTERING IS EASY
IF YOU TAKE THE TIME TO
PLAN AND DO IT NEATLY!

You can change the shape of the balloon to show different ways of speaking ...

or not speaking.

HELP!

Yelling

WHO ARE **YOU?**

Thinking

Cold and unfriendly

THE PRESIDENT THEN FELL OUT OF HIS CHAIR AND RIPPED HIS PANTS...

Radio or TV

Chapter 7

Drawing a Cartoon Scene

So, you see something funny happen and flash! the cartoonist inside you says, "Hey, that would make a <u>really</u> funny cartoon! (You can probably see how you could make it even funnier.) Well, you now have all the skills you need to draw that scene you see in your mind! Just as cartoon characters start with lightly penciled basic shapes, a cartoon scene starts with lightly penciled rough sketches. Let's walk through my 10 easy steps from a draft to a <u>great</u> finished cartoon.

For one cartoon, I did four thumbnail sketches to help me decide the best way to arrange the characters, the furniture, and the props to get my message across to the audience.

Which thumbnail do you think is the best one?

I chose this composition because people who speak English read from left to right and from top to bottom. In my final cartoon, your eye first sees the kids, then it moves down to the guys on the couch, and then you see the back of the TV. Finally, you read the caption, and it all makes sense (and, I hope, you laugh!).

"Their parents upstairs don't let them watch this show."

10 Easy Steps to Great Cartoons from Rough to .....

1. Gather your materials: pencil, eraser, ink pen, correction fluid, ruler, and drawing paper. Then, find a clean, quiet workspace.

2. Measure the size of your drawing area; in pencil draw the borders *lightly* on your final piece of paper. HINT: Make it big — it's easier to draw that way.

Let's say you want to draw a cartoon about a dinosaur in a swimming pool ...

3. On scrap paper, do a series of thumbnail sketches to work out the *composition* and *content* of your cartoon.

4. On your good paper, sketch *lightly* the basic shapes of your cartoon — characters, lettering, balloons, props, etc.

there's more ...

5. Erase and redraw the rough draft until it looks the way you want.

6. Add any texture, sound, and special effects that you want.

7. Ink over the best pencil lines — the ones you want to be a part of your finished cartoon.

8. Ink in the borders and other straight lines *using a ruler.*

9. After the ink dries, erase all pencil marks. Use correction fluid and your pen to correct any mistakes.

10. Sign your work! After all, it's a one-of-a-kind original!

Here are some ways I played around with my name:

First, I tried graphic styles.

Next, I tried some different lettering effects.

Finally, I looked at different ways to sign naturally.

(Guess which one I finally picked?)

★ **R**emember, it's <u>your</u> signature, so it can look however <u>you</u> want!

RUN!

AAAAH!

WHERE DID EVERYBODY GO??

EEK! A DINOSAUR!

Here's the finished product — a neat, clean cartoon that's worthy of being framed! You can give cartoons as gifts, or submit them for publication in books, magazines, and newspapers (see page 60).

finished!

Showing Your Stuff!

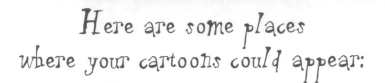

Here are some places
where your cartoons could appear:

School newspaper or newsletter	Church or temple bulletin
Community newspaper	Greeting cards
Neighborhood newsletter	Calendar
Classroom bulletin	Magazines
Signs in store windows	Website

I started out this way: I created a neighborhood newspaper, copied it at my dad's work, and gave it out to all our neighbors. At school, I offered to draw for the newspaper, for the weekly bulletin, for the yearbook — any place where people would like to see a cartoon or two. Soon, I was drawing for the local paper, too! I drew a comic strip every week for a local newspaper, for <u>10 years</u>!

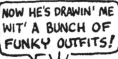

WELL, I ASKED FER IT, I HAD T' ASK FER DIFFERENT THREADS!

NOW HE'S DRAWIN' ME WIT' A BUNCH OF FUNKY OUTFITS!

AM I DOOMED NOW T' SUFFER TH' WHIMS OF A CRAZY CARTOONIST?

WILL YA STOP IT W' TH' GOOFY CLOTHES!

OH, NO !!

© 1985 Don Mayne

CREATING YOUR OWN COMIC STRIP

First, you decide on the characters — are they animal, human, or something else entirely? What are their personalities like? If they have very different personalities so that they sometimes annoy each other (hmm … like you and your younger brother, maybe?), you'll have loads of opportunities for funny situations.

Suzee's Room was a comic strip that I created with my daughter, Fiona. She was 12 years old at the time, and I let her draw the cartoon after I had done the sketching. (There are many comic strips that are worked on by more than one person.)

Cartooning in Cyberspace

Cartoons can add a whole new dimension to the fun you can have in cyberspace.

A computer and a scanner are awesome tools for a cartoonist. A scanner can reduce, enlarge, and stretch your cartoon, or you can work with the image in a graphics program to add color, photos, animation, and even special effects! With a scanner, you can post your own cartoons on the World Wide Web so that anyone, anywhere in the world, can see them! Pretty cool, huh?

"Spot" Cartoons

Look around — you'll see spot drawings everywhere. On billboards, advertisements, flyers, bulletins, books, magazine articles — just about anything that's printed on paper looks better with a cartoon! Spot cartoons are a great opportunity to show your stuff.

A spot drawing tries to capture the reader's attention, illustrate the story (or whatever it goes with), and it often tries to be funny, too!

"Faster, Dad! We're losing the picture!!"

Quick Starts CARTOONING SECRETS . . .

Draw what you like. Draw what you think is funny. If you never want to show anyone else, that's okay (your cartoons can be like your private journal). Or, share your drawings with millions of people, if you like!

The important thing is to KEEP ON DRAWING! And

HAVE FUN!

INDEX ✰ ✰ ✰

✰ ✰ ✰

More Good Books from WILLIAMSON PUBLISHING

Quick Starts for Kids! ® books for ages 8 to adult
are each 64 pages, fully illustrated, trade paper, 8½ x 11, $8.95 US/$10.95 CAN.

DRAWING HORSES
(that look real!)
by Don Mayne

KIDS' EASY BIKE CARE
Tune-Ups, Tools & Quick Fixes
by Steve Cole

ALMOST-INSTANT SCRAPBOOKS
by Laura Check

MAKE MAGIC!
50 Tricks to Mystify & Amaze
by Ron Burgess

40 KNOTS TO KNOW
Hitches, Loops, Bends & Bindings
by Emily Stetson

Dr. Toy 10 Best Socially Responsible Products
Dr. Toy 100 Best Children's Products
MAKE YOUR OWN BIRDHOUSES & FEEDERS
by Robyn Haus

GARDEN FUN!
Indoors & Out; In Pots & Small Spots
by Vicky Congdon

American Bookseller Pick of the Lists
MAKE YOUR OWN TEDDY BEARS & BEAR CLOTHES
by Sue Mahren

AND MORE:

Williamson's Kids Can! ® books for ages 7 to 14
are each 120 to 176 pages, fully illustrated,
trade paper, 11 x 8½, $12.95 US/$19.95 CAN.

Parents' Choice Recommended
KIDS' ART WORKS!
Creating with Color, Design, Texture & More
by Sandi Henry

Benjamin Franklin Best Education/Teaching Gold Award
Parent's Guide Children's Media Award
HAND-PRINT ANIMAL ART
by Carolyn Carreiro

Parents' Choice Gold Award
American Bookseller Pick of the Lists
THE KIDS' MULTICULTURAL ART BOOK
Art & Craft Experiences from Around the World
by Alexandra M. Terzian

REALLY COOL FELT CRAFTS
by Peg Blanchette & Terri Thibault

Parents' Choice Approved
BAKE THE BEST-EVER COOKIES!
by Sarah A. Williamson

BE A CLOWN!
Techniques from a Real Clown
by Ron Burgess

YO-YO!
Tips & Tricks from a Pro
by Ron Burgess

MAKE YOUR OWN CHRISTMAS ORNAMENTS
by Ginger Johnson

MAKE YOUR OWN FUN PICTURE FRAMES!
by Matt Phillips

KIDS' EASY KNITTING PROJECTS
by Peg Blanchette

KIDS' EASY QUILTING PROJECTS
by Terri Thibault

MAKE YOUR OWN HAIRWEAR
Beaded Barrettes, Clips, Dangles & Headbands
by Diane Baker

VISIT OUR WEBSITE!
www.williamsonbooks.com